Read·A·Picture

ANIMALS

By Burton Marks
Illustrated by Paul Harvey

JOSHUA MORRIS PUBLISHING

THE ANIMALS' PARTY

I'm having a party this afternoon and you're all invited.

HOORAY!

HOORAY!

HOORAY!

"But what will we wear?" said Benny the .

"I'll wear my striped ," said Gary the .

"I'll wear my straw ," said Cora the .

"I'll wear my blue ," said Felix the .

"We'll wear our wool ," said 3 smiling .

"I'll wear my silk ," said Millie the .

"I'll wear a , of course," said Harold the .

"We'll wear our red ," said 2 little .

"We'll wear our new ," said the twin .

And that is just what they did.

LOOK AT ME

Look at me! Look at me!
See all the things that I can be.

I can be an   ,

I can be a   ,

or I can be a

and prowl about the   .

I can be a   ,

I can be a   ,

or I can be a

and fly high in the air.

I can be a

and swing among the  .

When I play make-believe
I can be anything I please.

PICTURE A RIDDLE

- What is the safest kind of lion to have around the house?

- What kind of dog do you see at football games?

- What kind of key opens bananas?

- What would you get if you cross a pig with a pine tree?

- What animal complains the most?

TOPSY-TURVY TOWN

Did you ever hear a  meow

or see a polka-dotted  ?

Strange things like that are all around
in crazy Topsy-Turvy Town.

 are smooth as silk

and billy  give chocolate milk.

 laugh, hyenas frown

in silly Topsy-Turvy Town.

are as small as

and are twice the size of .

don't sting and don't moo

and cock-a-doodle-doo .

 do not make a sound,

and  live underground.

 are green and  are brown

in mixed-up Topsy-Turvy Town.

 can swim and  can fly,

but please don't ever ask me why.
Because *everything* is upside down
in crazy Topsy-Turvy Town.

WHAT A SHOW!

When the animals put on a show

I hop on my  and off I go.

I laugh when I see the dance,

and clap my as the prance.

The  and

fly through the air;

and a  drives a

with a grizzly

In all the 🌍
there are few things I know
that are $\frac{1}{2}$ as much fun
as an animal show!

PICTURE A RIDDLE

•What animal are you when you take a bath?

•What does Lassie plant in her garden?

•What animal are you when you're just too tired to move?

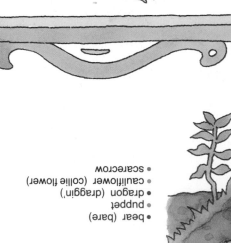

•What kind of pet dances and sings?

•What kind of crow keeps birds away?

• bear (bare)
• puppet
• dragon (draggin')
• cauliflower (collie flower)
• scarecrow

MY GARDEN GUEST

Pretty little

flying through the pale blue sky,

I can't belicve that once you were

a fuzzy wuzzy  .

POOR KANGAROO

"What will I do?" said  .

"I cannot find my other 👟 .

My (scarf) and (hat) are missing, too.

Where can they be? I wish I knew.

There's something funny going on—

my ⚽ is also gone;

my purple (socks) , my teddy (bear) ,

I cannot find them anywhere.
Where can they be? I've not a clue—
have you?"

Can you help Kangaroo
find his socks and missing shoe?
Can you also help him find his hat,
his bear, his scarf, and his football?

ANIMAL TALK

"Good morning," I said to the animals. "I hope you have a nice day."

The  said, "Gobble, gobble."

The replied, "Neigh, neigh."

The  said, "Bow-wow."

"Moo, moo," said the

The 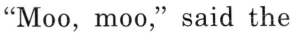 said, "Cluck, cluck."

"Quack, quack," said the

The  said, "Cheep, cheep."

The said, "Cock-a-doodle-doo."

"Baa, baa," said the 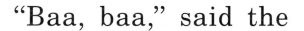 .

And the wise old  said, "Whoooo?"

And I said, "It's been very nice talking with you."

PICTURE A RIDDLE

- What animal are you when you're not telling the truth?

- What's the best thing to do if you see a snowball coming towards you?

- What kind of fish twinkles?

- What is the largest kind of ant?

- What animal are you when you have a frog in your throat?

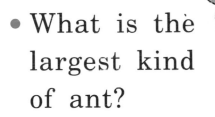

- lion (lyin')
- giant
- starfish
- duck
- horse (hoarse)

Goodbe and farewell.

We put the U had

fun reading this book.